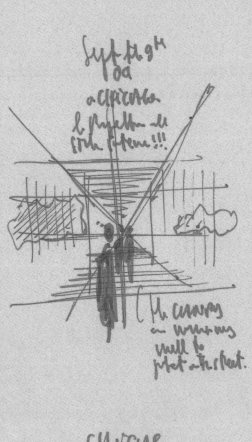

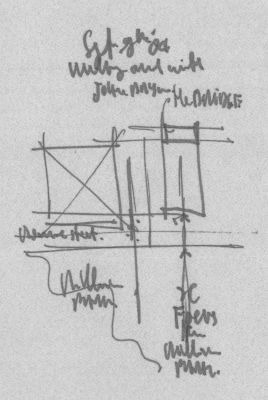

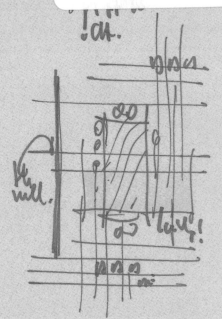

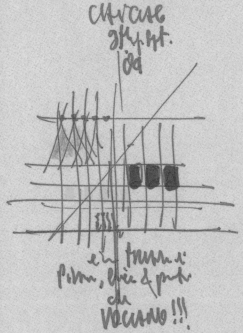

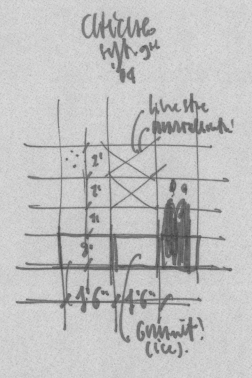

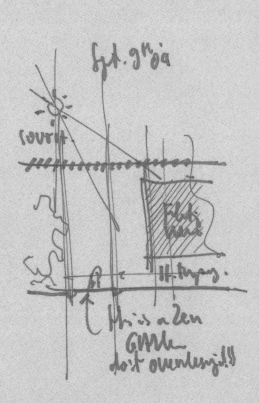

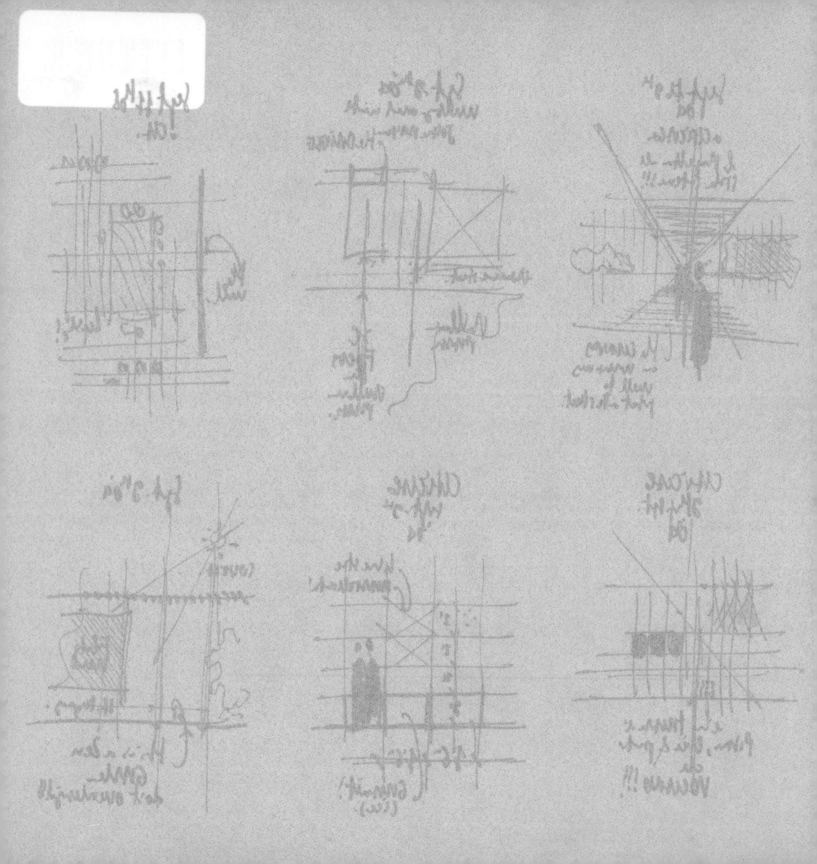

ZERO GRAVITY

The Art Institute
Renzo Piano
Building for a
New Century

THE ART INSTITUTE OF CHICAGO

James Cuno

Martha Thorne

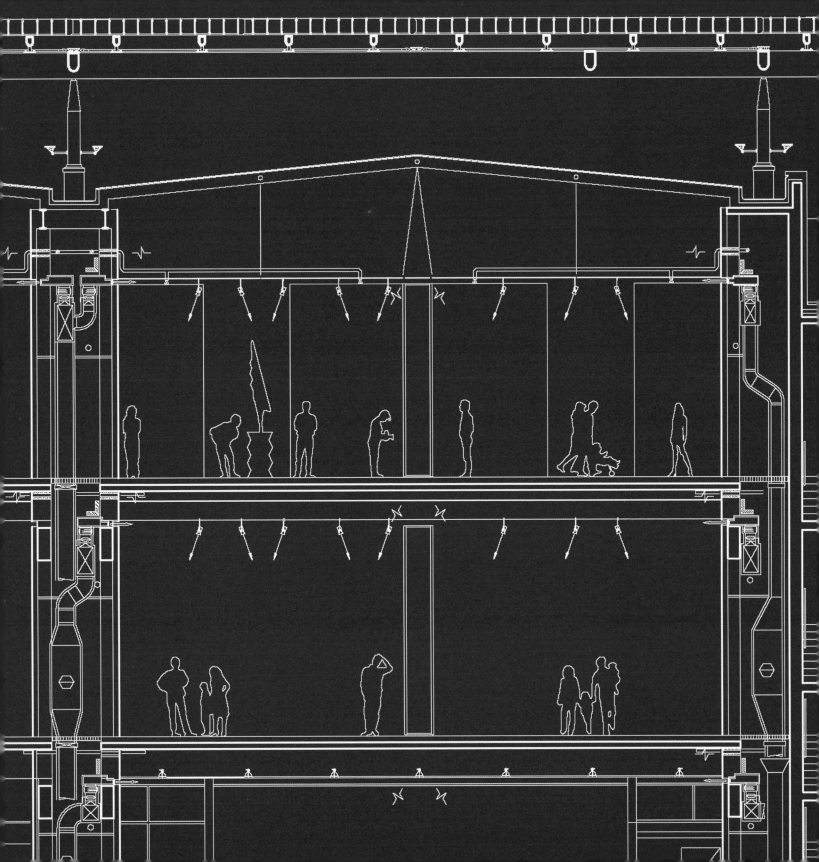

AN ARCHITECT SPENDS HIS LIFE FIGHTING against gravity and, believe me, gravity is the most stubborn law of nature.

To be honest, the architect's job also consists in discovering the roots of the place he is building in. Architecture is, in fact, the most *local* of the arts: you have to dig, to seize the *topos*, and to hold it tight.

But then you have to struggle against gravity; you have to leave the ground to give air and lightness to your work.

Because architecture must fly: it is made of emotions, tensions, transparency.

These two dimensions, the air and the ground, are present in the project for the Art Institute of Chicago.

On one hand, the building is deeply rooted into the ground and represents a natural continuation of what is already there: the same stone and same mass.

On the other hand, the huge "flying carpet" that protects the third-floor galleries from direct sunlight and the gentle arc of the bridge that links the new building to Millennium Park express lightness, transparency, and the scheme's connection to the world of nature.

ZERO GRAVITY

Renzo Piano

I CAME TO THE ART INSTITUTE IN AUGUST 2004, when construction drawings for the museum's new north wing were nearly finished. The project had been conceived and developed by my predecessor, James N. Wood. He commissioned a future site development and master plan from Skidmore, Owings and Merrill in 1996 and led a small team in the selection of Renzo Piano as the architect of the new addition to the museum. He won support from the Art Institute's Board of Trustees and worked to define the program, quality, and character of the desired architecture. In so many ways, this is Jim's endeavor. I had the simple good fortune to come along when I did.

I had worked with Renzo Piano for many years on a building for the Harvard University Art Museums. At one stage, I gathered a few trusted colleagues together with significant supporters to critique the project. Jim was one of those colleagues.

Over the years, Jim and I would talk about our respective development plans: his was advancing while mine was going in circles. I heard a lot about the Art Institute's project during that time. And when Jim announced his retirement and I was chosen to succeed him, I could not have been more pleased. I have the highest regard for Jim, for his leadership of the Art Institute, for the Art Institute itself, and for Renzo and the work of the Renzo Piano Building Workshop. I am convinced of the importance of this building to the museum, to Chicago, and even to Renzo's architectural practice. It will be the largest museum designed by him to date and will undoubtedly hold a prominent place in the history and cultural life of the city.

Since I've been involved, we have made a few changes: we refined the program to dedicate the new north wing exclusively to modern and contemporary painting, sculpture,

FOREWORD AND ACKNOWLEDGMENTS

James Cuno
President and Eloise W. Martin Director

photography, film and video, and architecture; modified some galleries; and added the bridge between Millennium Park and the rooftop dining facility and sculpture terrace. Otherwise, the project is as Jim left it.

The publication of this small book, along with the exhibition that it accompanies, was occasioned by our breaking ground on May 31, 2005. Construction is intended to last three years. With a fourth year to commission the building and install the collections, we intend to open the new wing in spring 2009.

Many people have helped with this project, far too many to mention everyone by name. I should acknowledge a few key individuals, however. John H. Bryan, Chairman of the Board of Trustees; Louis Susman, Trustee and Chairman of the Capital Campaign; and Andrew M. Rosenfield, Vice Chairman of the Board and Chairman of the Project Oversight Committee, have guided us to the groundbreaking with confidence, enthusiasm, and optimism for the future. Patricia A. Woodworth, the Art Institute's Executive Vice President for Finance and Administration and Chief Financial Officer; Edward W. Horner, Jr.,

TOP Design meeting in the offices of Renzo Piano Building Workshop with Renzo Piano (seated, left), Joost Moolhuijzen, and Dominique Rat (standing)
ABOVE Former Art Institute director James N. Wood with Joost Moolhuijzen

Executive Vice President for Development and Public Affairs; and Meredith Mack, Vice President for Finance and Operations, were and remain crucial members of the project team. The exhibition was organized by Martha Thorne, Associate Curator of Architecture, and designed by Joost Moolhuijzen and Dominique Rat of the Renzo Piano Building Workshop, and Joseph Cochand, the Art Institute's Senior Exhibition Designer. The catalogue was designed by Karin Kuzniar of the Department of Graphic Design, and Photographic and Communications Services, Lyn DelliQuadri, Executive Director. It was edited by Robert V. Sharp and Katherine E. Reilly and produced by Amanda W. Freymann of the Publications Department. Our many thanks go to each of these colleagues and to the many contributors to the Art Institute's capital campaign, "Building of the Century."

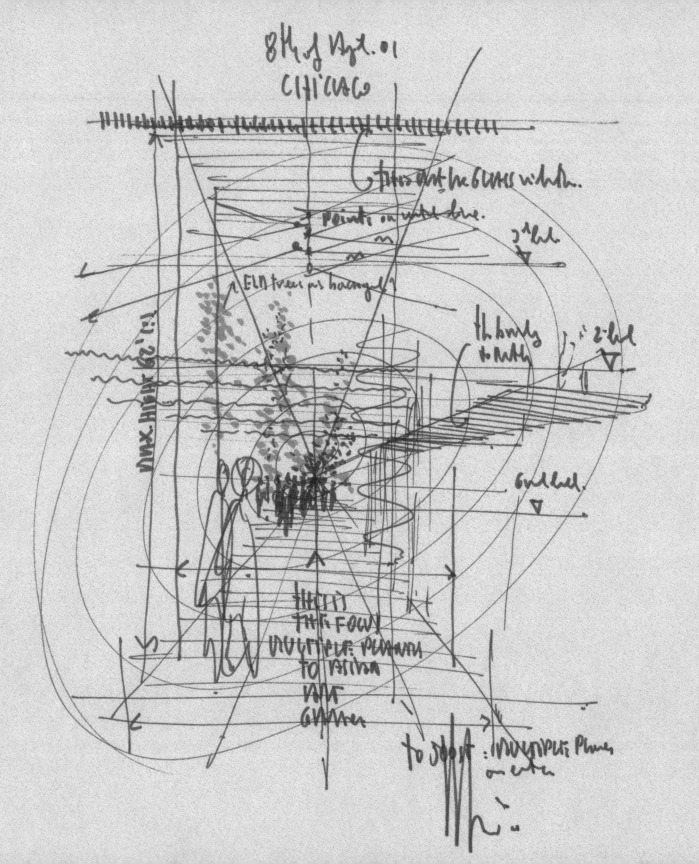

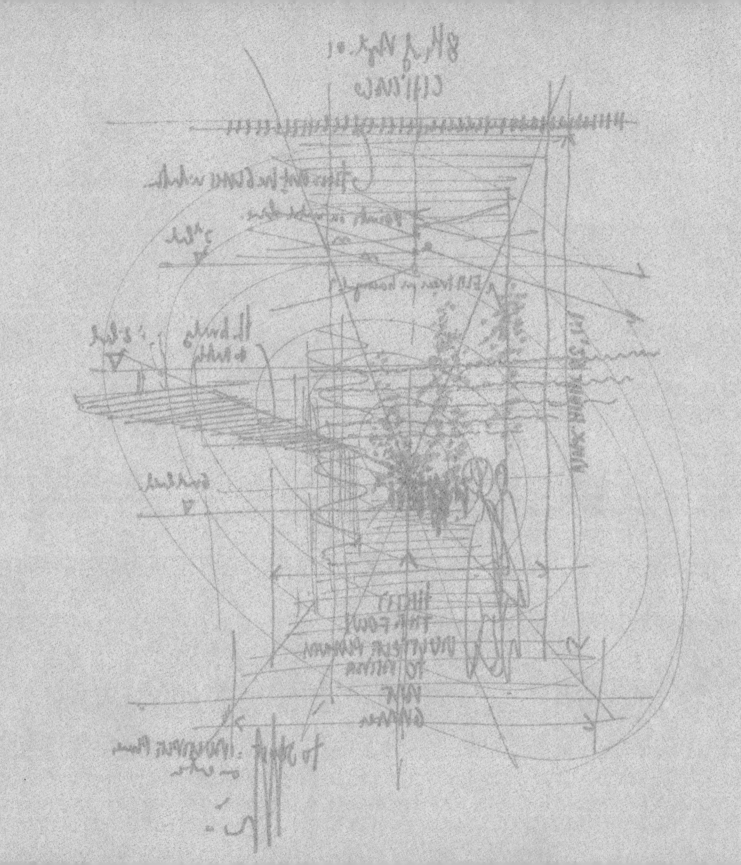

AT A CELEBRATORY DINNER, I ONCE introduced Richard Meier as the Apollo of contemporary architecture and Renzo Piano as its Dionysius. I was only half joking. Meier's architecture embodies rational thought. There is very little poetry or emotion, and very little sensuality. Surfaces are hard, angles unforgiving, light constant. Piano's architecture, on the other hand, is always changing: in its materials, form, and technology, and in its relation to the specific conditions of the site. He is famous for spending time walking the site before taking a job, and then walking it again every time he returns: to come to know its structural peculiarities, to be sure, but also its "sense of place." This is true even when there is no site, as was the case with Kansai International Airport in Osaka.

> Before entering the competition for Kansai, I asked the client what I always ask in these cases: to visit the site. There was a moment of embarrassment, because there was none. Japan is a very crowded country, and Osaka had no room for a new airport, so the relevant authorities decided to build it in the sea. . . . The client took the three of us, Peter Rice, Nori Okabe, and myself, on a boat trip that lasted an afternoon. "Where is the airport going to be?" asked Nori. . . . "Here," answered our guide. We were in the open sea. Castaways adrift on a raft—at least that was how we felt. We were lost in the infinite, drunk on space. So we started to look for something to hold onto outside the physical context: in the collective unconscious, in memory, in culture.[1]

Piano also drew, as he always does, on his own memories. He was born in Genoa by the Ligurian Sea, not far from where he now works in Punta Nave ("Ship Rock"), and near to where he docks his sailboat, an elegant craft of his own design. His many youthful walks along the sea have remained a vital source of his imagination. He says he loves the way the sea always changes in color and reflectivity, and in relative

FIGHTING GRAVITY/MAKING MAGIC:
RENZO PIANO AND THE ART INSTITUTE'S NEW NORTH WING

James Cuno

calm or sudden danger. It is both a source and a metaphor for how he works: in a light-filled space, open to the sky with a limitless view, encouraging of contemplation but also of sociability. It is a site of risk-taking and relentless experimentation in the context of a deep and abiding regard for tradition.

He says too that he loves the way the sea serves a purpose, as a bustling highway of commercial activity. He often looks up from his work desk to see tankers jockeying for position as they enter the port of Genoa. And of course he knows the port well from his many visits to it ever since he was a child (he also worked on a revitalization project there during the late 1980s).

> The light and the sea: for me, these two things together mean the port. The port is a powerful landscape made up of elements that are both grand and ephemeral, that are continually changing— reflections on the water, suspended loads, swiveling cranes, and of course ships coming and going. Who knows where that ship is coming from, in what direction it is headed?[2]

The business of the port, the noise, the smells, the rush of workers—all are reminiscent of the construction sites that his builder father took him to as a child. Often the two kinds of sites and memories merge when he talks of his profession.

> I still love building sites. They are wonderful places, where every- thing is in movement, where the landscape changes every day. They are a great human adventure. . . . The building site is always a place of extraordinary discoveries. . . .The process of construc- tion is never complete. . . . Buildings, like cities, are factories of the infinite and the unfinished.[3]

Such memories were stirred in the architect when he first walked the site for the new north wing of the Art Institute in 1996. To the east was the sea-sized Lake Michigan, with its sailboat harbor snug along the shore and, in the distance, a line of ships filled with industrial cargo bound for the port of Chicago. To the north was the construction site of what would become Millennium Park, with its millions of happy visitors playing in the Crown Fountain, walking the Lurie Garden paths, or listening to music swelling from the ribbonlike titanium forms of Frank Gehry's Pritzker Pavilion (see fig. 1). And then beyond, to the west and north, rising along Michigan Avenue and Randolph Street, were skyscrap- ers, the building form with which the city of Chicago is so firmly identified in history. And then, too, running right through the center of the site was a railway, with metal cars shuttling back and forth carrying commuters north in the morning, south in the evening. It was the perfect Chicago setting: a blend of commerce, transportation, culture, and lakeshore. It must have seemed a lot like Genoa, without the salt air.

At first there was talk of building across the railroad tracks south of Gunsaulus Hall between the Morton Wing and the Rice Building. But the difficulties of such construction, together with a desire to balance circulation within the museum and to respond to the emerging, compelling presence of Millennium Park, caused the Art Institute to shift its attention to the abandoned Goodman Theatre site to the northeast, on the corner of Monroe Street and Columbus Drive (fig. 2). Here the new building could take full advantage of light from the north and offer visitors breathtaking views of the park and the skyline of the city through north-facing gallery windows. It was a perfect site to build a stand-alone building—a new north wing—roughly equivalent in size to the combined volume of the Rice and School of the Art Institute buildings, with easy access for visitors and groups off Columbus Drive, and just across Monroe Street from Millennium Park and its new parking garage.

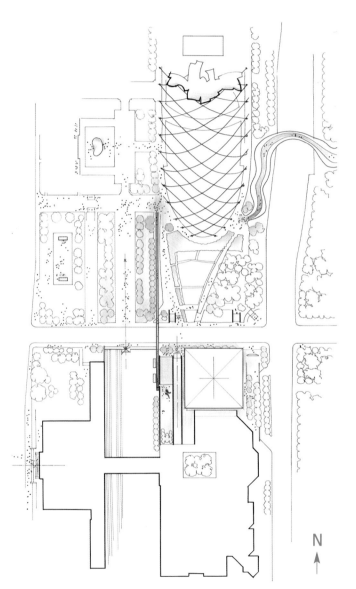

9

N

FIG. 1 Site plan showing the Art Institute campus, including the new north wing, and Millennium Park to the north

But the site was visually cacophonous at best. Green spaces lay to the north and east, railway tracks to the west, and various styles and ages of limestone construction to the south. The Art Institute had been almost in perpetual construction and renovation since its first building opened on the current location in 1893. It grew first more densely within its original footprint, and then in the second decade of the twentieth century it spanned the railway tracks with a two-story gallery bridge (Gunsaulus Hall). A few years later, galleries were added east of the tracks, connecting Gunsaulus Hall with the recently constructed McKinlock Court. Other structures were built during the middle decades of the century: the B. F. Ferguson Memorial Building in 1958; the Morton Wing in 1962; a new building for the School of the Art Institute, Rubloff Auditorium, the Columbus Drive entrance, and enclosed galleries around McKinlock Court from 1974 to 1978; and the Daniel F. and Ada L. Rice Building in 1988. Piano's great challenge was how to add yet one more—and one *very large*—building to this assemblage of diverse, even divergent, and in one case, markedly eccentric, architectural styles.

This is just the kind of problem Piano likes. After all, he hails from one of the most densely built cities in Europe.

He understands how to add to and intervene in such conditions with sensitivity, elegance, and modesty. He has been doing this for much of his career, and he always begins with the site. And not just with its physical characteristics, but with what he call its "ecology": how it is sited, how much and what quality of light it gets, what its structures are made of, how it is used, what its history is, how it is regarded within the city, what its program is to be, and what the ambitions of its occupants, his client, are.

> Every place is different, every client is different, every society is different. Culturally, historically, psychologically, anthropologically, and topographically, every job is different. . . . I never take a new job without visiting the place, without trying to understand, without trying to get a basic, fundamental emotion. Because that's what it's all about—building emotion. I try to understand what is the real nature of a place, what is the context. . . . Architecture is not an art independent from reality. Real architecture, real painting, real poetry, real music is never detached from physicality. In architecture, that's it. Architecture is at the edge, between art and anthropology, between society and science, technology and history. Sometimes memory, too, plays a part. Architecture is about illusion and symbolism, semantics, and the art of telling stories. It's a funny mixture of these things. Sometimes it's humanistic and sometimes it's materialistic.[4]

His answer, as it turned out, was deceptively simple. He has designed a building that comprises three attached elements above grade—a three-story east pavilion for galleries and museum education; a three-story west pavilion for galleries, visitor services, and boardrooms; and a double-height circulation spine that connects the two pavilions and leads the visitor into the rest of the museum (see fig. 4 and pls. 3–7). These are joined below grade by a common basement for storage, work rooms, a loading dock, and mechanical systems. The east pavilion is divided vertically into three bays, with vertical circulation elements on the east exterior. Hovering over much of this new construction, and extending south over a large portion of a new garden court that will lie between the pavilion and Rubloff Auditorium, is a metallic-colored extruded aluminum canopy (Piano has dubbed it a "flying carpet") that captures the north light and delivers it to the third-floor gallery skylights while gently shading the garden (see pl. 14).

The circulation spine directs people into the new building from Monroe Street on the north and McKinlock Court on the south. On entering the spine

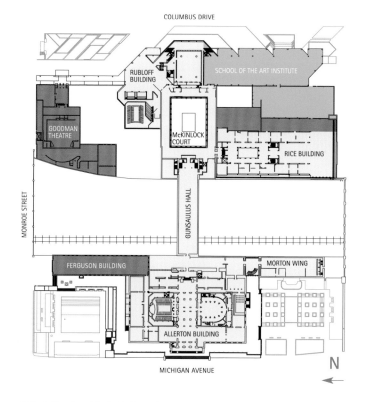

FIG. 2 Site plan of the Art Institute prior to addition of the new north wing

11

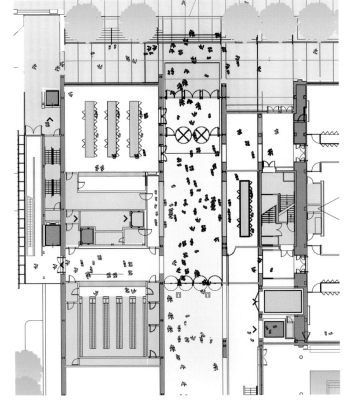

from the north, visitors are introduced to the Art Institute, can purchase tickets and items from the retail shop, give up their outerwear to a cloakroom attendant, and turn into a series of classrooms and meeting spaces for museum education (see fig. 3). Piano calls this the "profane" part of the building, an initial decompression zone outside the museum's security perimeter in which one begins to prepare for the experience of the galleries, or the "sacred" part of the building (he calls the entrance area the place where one "takes off one's shoes," as in a Japanese house or temple). Then one either continues down this "main street" (see fig. 5) and deeper into the building, or rises up to the two floors of galleries that constitute the major component of the new wing.

The new building is dedicated to the Art Institute's modern and contemporary collections: paintings, sculpture, photography, film and video, and architecture. (Modern, but not contemporary, American painting and sculpture will remain with earlier American art in the Rice Building.) The galleries off the spine at grade will display rotating installations from the photography collection (to the east) and temporary

FIG. 3 Partial first-floor plan showing new entrance on Monroe Street, shop, ticket counters, and cloakroom

12

exhibitions relevant to any of the collections shown elsewhere in the new building (to the west). Stairs set elegantly before a two-story glass wall overlooking the new garden court will lead visitors to the galleries above (see figs. 6–7). From the second-floor landing they can turn northward into the east pavilion's galleries of contemporary art and rise again to view modern art on the third floor (see plans, pp. 49–51). Retracing their steps along the landing, they can enter galleries on the east devoted to film and video and installation art and on the west to architecture. At this point, visitors can leave the new building and enter the second floor of Gunsaulus Hall, proceeding through installations of European painting, sculpture, and decorative art.

In this way, the north wing not only will add approximately 65,000 square feet of new gallery space and around 20,000 square feet for classrooms and conference rooms, but also will help clarify the visitor's experience. Every curatorial department in the entire museum will gain gallery space as a result of the project, and new and more coherent installations will aid in the understanding of various narratives in

FIG. 4 Model of new north wing addition, showing the east pavilion, glass-enclosed central concourse, and west pavilion, in an aerial view from the north

FIG. 5 View of model down "main street," looking south

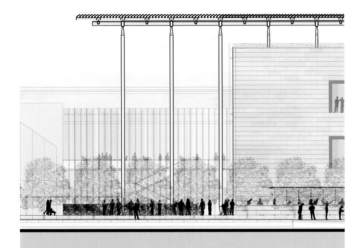

FIG. 6 Portion of the Columbus Drive elevation showing the location of new garden court (detail of pl. 3)

FIG. 7 Perspective view of the garden court between the east pavilion and Rubloff Auditorium

the history of the world's art as told through the Art Institute's collections. The McKinlock Court galleries on the first level will be dedicated to Southeast Asian and ancient Mediterranean art, connecting to galleries of African, Amerindian, Islamic, and East Asian art on the lower level of Gunsaulus Hall and the Morton Wing. The arts of Europe, from the medieval period through the nineteenth century, will be located on the second floor of Gunsaulus Hall, the Allerton Building, and the Morton Wing (see fig. 2). Regenstein Hall will remain our principal facility for major temporary exhibitions, and the galleries of the Rice Building will be dedicated to American art, while those on the lower level of McKinlock Court and the Rice Building will house decorative arts and textiles. New galleries for prints and drawings will be developed on the first floor of Allerton next to the Goldman Study Center.

The intention behind this reconfiguration of galleries is a clarity of curatorial narrative that will enhance the visitor's experience of the entire Art Institute, which, as in the case of every large museum, can be difficult and tiring. Engaging with works of art is demanding. It takes time and requires a great deal of standing and walking. Closed spaces and artificial light can make this worse. Piano is very concerned with this and has made light and transparency a hallmark of his museum architecture. From the Menil Collection of 1987 to the Beyeler Foundation Museum of 1997 and the Nasher Sculpture Center of 2003 (see the essay by Martha Thorne, pp. 35–46), he has designed views from galleries out on to nature and experimented relentlessly with ways of capturing and filtering natural light. Constant artificial light takes life from a room. It is never as nourishing as sunlight, which is ever changing: bright and white one moment, soft and blue the next; now focused, then diffused, then focused again. Natural light reminds us of the time of day and the character of the weather. In Chicago, by the lake, with wind and starkly contrasting seasons, daylight takes on myriad qualities. Chicagoans depend on this. It is characteristic of the place and of their sense of place. They like to walk outside, particularly along the lake and in Daniel Burnham's lakefront parks.

Piano acknowledges this in his design for the new north wing. Everywhere visitors have views onto nature: the garden court seen from the circulation spine and the upper landing between galleries; Millennium Park seen through the north-facing glass curtain wall; and always the sky and clouds seen through skylights. This is meant to humanize the experience of visiting the museum, to encourage slowing down and taking refreshment from the surroundings, literally to be *inspired* (from the Latin *inspiro*, to breathe upon). And then, too, he has designed an ascent by elevator within a glass circulation spine on the exterior wall of the west pavilion, up to a glass-enclosed dining facility and an outdoor sculpture terrace with views to the east across Grant Park to the lake, to Michigan Avenue, and to the western edge of Millennium Park (see fig. 9). Here visitors will take stock of their experience of the museum as was intended by the Art Institute's founders: as a civic institution in the center of the city; at the nexus of public transportation; amidst residential, cultural, and commercial buildings, bustling parks, and the thriving lakeshore. It is not removed to the margins of city life, not a hermitage withdrawn into its own world, but a crossroads of the world's great cultures for all Chicagoans, a source of local, regional, and national pride, and a testament to the spirit of the city as articulated by Daniel Burnham and Edward Bennett in their *Plan of Chicago* in 1909:

> This spirit—the spirit of Chicago—is our greatest asset. It is not merely civic pride: it is rather the constant, steady determination to bring about the very best conditions of city life for all the peo-

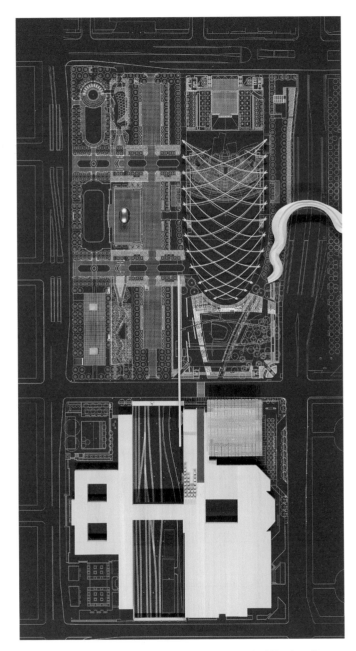

FIG. 8 Collage showing the Art Institute campus with the pedestrian bridge that will run from the third floor of the west pavilion well into Millennium Park

ple, with full knowledge that what we as a people decide to do in the public interest we can and surely will bring to pass.[5]

After taking in the view, visitors will be able descend by escalator back into the museum or stroll down the long, elegant bridge across Monroe Street and into Millennium Park (see pl. 6).

The bridge (see fig. 8) is an important aspect of the north wing project. It completes the natural path of circulation—in from Michigan Avenue, through the museum, out to the park, and back on to Michigan Avenue—and emphasizes the Art Institute's location on the street, smack in the center of the city. There will be two main entrances: one on Michigan Avenue and another on Monroe Street opposite the park. The former rear entrance, off Columbus Drive, turned its back to the city. It was always a secondary door, used primarily by school groups, bus tours, and visitors who drove in from out of town and parked in nearby garages. It was not a natural entrance for people walking along Michigan Avenue, who might want to come into the Art Institute for a minute to see a favorite painting, an hour to see an exhibition, or an entire day to see the permanent collection. There was something always forlorn about the Columbus Drive entrance. It did not present a warm welcome to the visitor. It was too obviously the back door.

The north wing, with its door on axis with the gardens and the Pritzker Pavilion of Millennium Park, and with its elegant bridge physically connecting the museum and the park, will be a true second—and not a *secondary*—entrance for the Art Institute. Many times of the year, it will be just as busy as the Michigan Avenue entrance. Imagine the experience of walking slowly up the bridge from Millennium Park. Its vantage will allow views back to the band shell and over the Lurie Garden; west to the Crown Fountain and McCormick-Tribune Plaza and to Michigan Avenue with its varied facade, a living history of Chicago's skyscrapers; and east to the great blue expanse of the lake. Arriving on the roof of the north wing's west pavilion, one can see sculpture set against a backdrop of plantings, sky, and views of Millennium Park, and enter the dining facility with its views back to the city and out to the lake (see fig. 9). It will be a thrilling experience, a lesson in the history, beauty, and character of Chicago, and a reminder that the Art Institute is and always has been indelibly a part of this great city. Then, one can descend into the museum—for a minute, an hour, the day—and experience the world of art that it holds in trust for the public, as Chicago's Art Institute.

Piano is committed to the role of architecture in strengthening the bonds of civic life. And he understands the place of art museums in doing this. He has designed them for large cities (Paris, Centre Georges Pompidou) and neighborhoods (Houston, the Menil Collection), for suburbs (the Beyeler Foundation Museum outside of Basel, Switzerland) and gardens (the Nasher Sculpture Center in Dallas). And he has designed them for almost thirty years. He believes that the function of museums in public life has changed in that time. They are no longer the imposing institutions of the nineteenth and early twentieth centuries, nor the circuslike environments of the go-go years of the late twentieth century. His and Richard Rogers's Pompidou Center of 1978 (see Thorne, fig. 2) was just such a circus or "provocation," as he calls it, "a joyful urban machine." His museums ever since have been more modest in appearance: simple forms of stone and wood and, of course, light.

> Today, people speak of rediscovering art. They are looking for an easygoing relationship between the building (the architecture of the museum) and art. The public is interested in the relationship

17

of the museum and nature and in the resonance of light. This is not an abstract discussion as in architectural circles. People don't care at all about the architecture. I like this reaction.[6]

The Art Institute's new north wing building could not be simpler in appearance: a few, straight walls of Indiana limestone, reflecting the materials of the other buildings on the site, connected by steel and glass, mainly glass (see fig. 10). Its walls are like shifting planes—the bays of the east pavilion are equal in width to that of the west pavilion and are just under twice as wide as the central spine—with glass spanning the distances between them. The walls convey strength and solidity; it is important that they are strong. The building has to have presence, to hold its own among the earlier museum structures and to anchor its northeast corner. But it is equally important that the building is light.

An exhibition at the Museum of Modern Art in 1995 identified a resurgent interest in lightness among contemporary architects: lightness in form, structure, aesthetic, and environmental impact.[7] Piano was represented by his Kansai International Airport in Osaka. Elsewhere he described the lightness of that project's form symbolically as a "glider," evocative of the building's purpose.[8] The aerodynamic form did not have a purely symbolic value, however; it also served to make the building more energy efficient. In other words, Piano employed lightness as symbol and function. This was true also of his Tjibaou Cultural Center in Nouméa, New Caledonia, where vegetal roof forms soar above the forest canopy and recall indigenous architectural traditions while allowing for passive ventilation of the buildings.[9]

The light structure of the Art Institute's new north wing is also symbolic: the "flying carpet" canopy hovers over the building like a ship's rigging, the walls of shifting planes recall the trains moving back and forth on the tracks to the west, and the modernist design of glass and steel acknowledges the Miesian legacy of the second school of Chicago architecture. But it is also energy efficient. Maximizing and filtering natural light captured from the north reduces the call for artificial lighting, just as the opaque walls east and west and the canopy shading the south-facing windows of the east pavilion reduce the amount of heat gain in the building.

Piano is deeply concerned about these things. And he knows that they must all be, in the end, expressed through the poetry, elegance, and beauty of his design. Herbert Muschamp once said that Piano has "collapsed the divide between metaphor and material. . . . It has nothing to do with style but much to do with elegance, in the mathematical as well as the corporeal sense of that term. Seen in the context of his ideas, Piano can give lightness of being even to solid brick walls."[10] And, for Piano, this is an ethical issue. He believes that architecture is a form of civic responsibility. At its best, it enhances civic life with beauty, dignity, pleasure, and magic; gives form to its aspirations; and contributes to its economic and environmental sustainability. As he put it, "As an architect, I don't preach morality—I design it and build it, trying to maintain the profound nature of our profession, that of architecture as a service, as a project for the community."[11]

He does not preach morality, nor is he a preacher. He is a man of great charm and humor who can still, after decades of working with powerful commercial and governmental clients, find a source of childlike innocence and pleasure in making things. He confesses that he loves to spend time in his model-maker's workshop, touching things and playing with them. And at work in the studio he surrounds himself with them: fragments from models of various

FIG. 9 View to the north from the rooftop sculpture terrace
FIG. 10 Portion of the Monroe Street elevation showing the glass curtain wall (detail of pl. 4)

projects suspended from the ceiling, tacked to the wall, and sitting on tables. "What I do is mentally I touch each one," he once said. "They're like my children, and I go and touch each one to understand what is going on."[12]

There is something profoundly sensual in the way Piano works, and in the results of his work. That is why I said I was only half joking when I introduced him once as the Dionysius of contemporary architecture. For as he himself said: "I like fighting gravity. Magic is essential in architecture. . . . complexity comes from texture, from vibration, from the metamorphic capacity of the building to transform, to change, to breathe. Sometimes buildings even make sounds."[13] Would Apollo ever have said that?

NOTES

1. Renzo Piano, *The Renzo Piano Logbook*, trans. Huw Evans (Thames and Hudson, 1997), p. 150.

2. Ibid., pp. 15–16.

3. Ibid., p. 14.

4. Interview with Architectural Record, http://archrecord.construction.com/people/interviews/archives/0110piano.asp.

5. Daniel H. Burnham and Edward H. Bennett, *Plan of Chicago* (1909; rpt. Princeton Architectural Press, 1993), p. 8.

6. Interview with Lutz Windhöfel, "Creating Silence," in *Renzo Piano: Fondation Beyeler; A Home for Art* (Birkhäuser, 1998), p. 31.

7. Terence Riley, *Light Construction*, exh. cat. (Museum of Modern Art, 1995).

8. *The Renzo Piano Logbook* (note 1), p. 152.

9. Peter Buchanan, *Renzo Piano Building Workshop: Complete Works*, vol. 4 (Phaidon, 2000), pp. 86–117.

10. Herbert Muschamp, "Lessons of a Humanist Who Can Disturb the Peace," *New York Times*, July 14, 2002, http://www.nytimes.com/.

11. *The Renzo Piano Logbook* (note 1), p. 13.

12. Interview with Architectural Record (note 4).

13. Ibid.

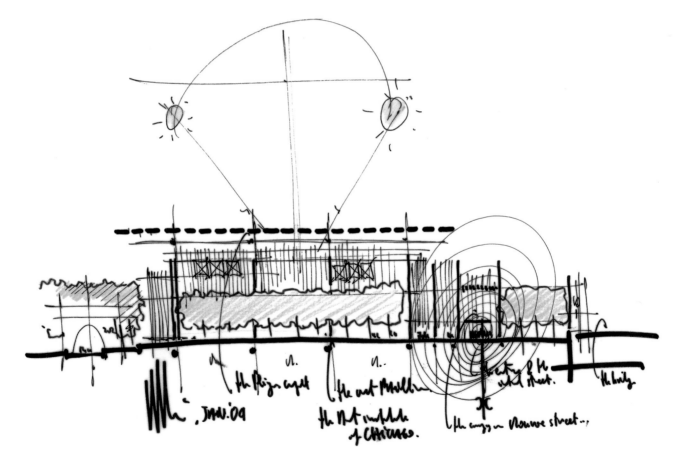

1. Sketch of Monroe Street elevation of the new north wing

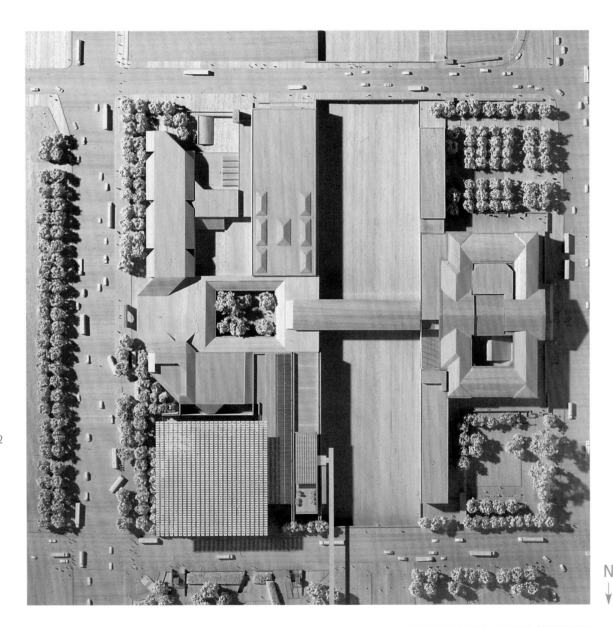

2. Aerial view of model showing entire Art Institute campus, including the new north wing

N
↓

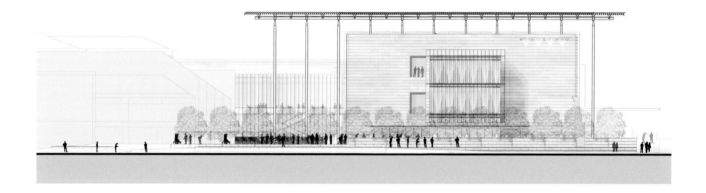

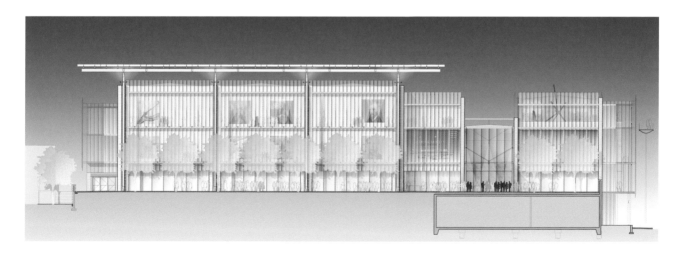

3 . Columbus Drive, or east, elevation
4 . Monroe Street, or north, elevation

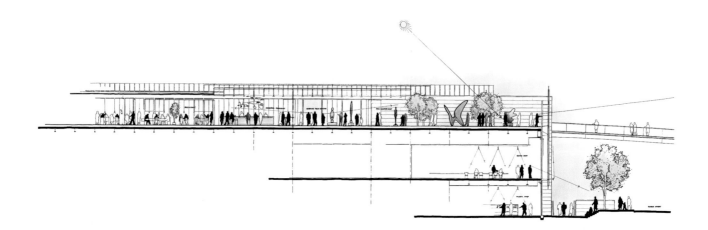

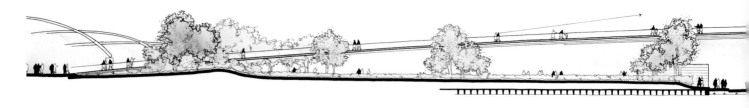

5. North–south section through the dining facility and sculpture terrace on the third floor of the west pavilion, looking east

6. West elevation showing the pedestrian bridge from Millennium Park to the new north wing

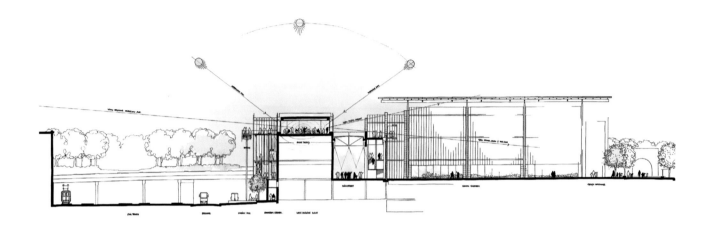

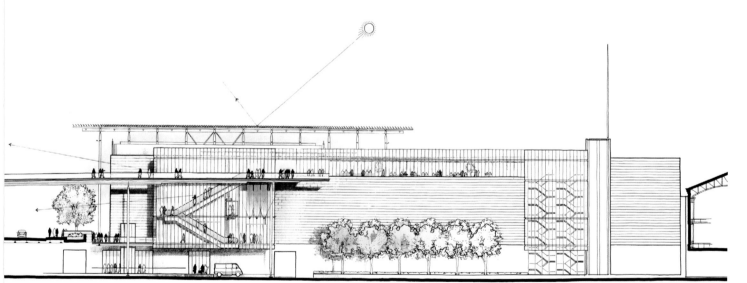

7. East–west section through the dining facility and "main street," looking north

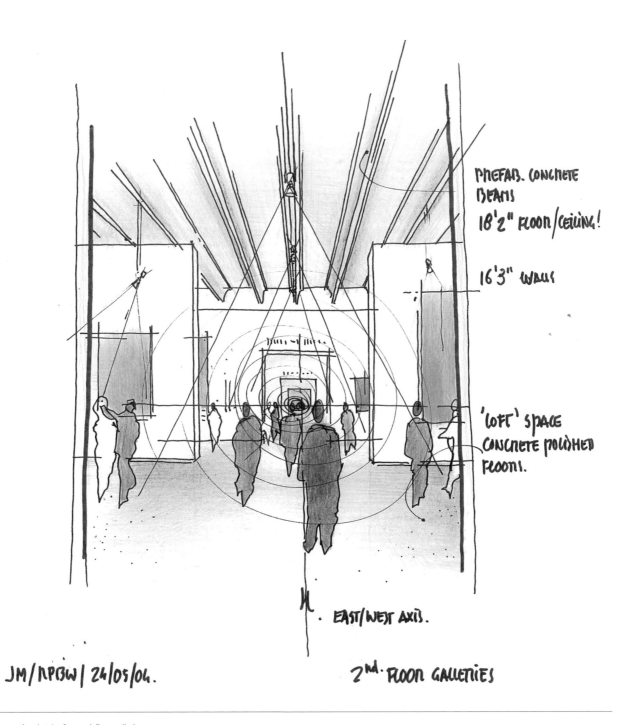

PREFAB. CONCRETE
BEAMS
18'2" FLOOR/CEILING!

16'3" WALLS

'LOFT' SPACE
CONCRETE POLISHED
FLOORS.

EAST/WEST AXIS.

JM/RPBW/ 24/05/04.

2ⁿᵈ· FLOOR GALLERIES

10. Perspective sketch of second-floor galleries

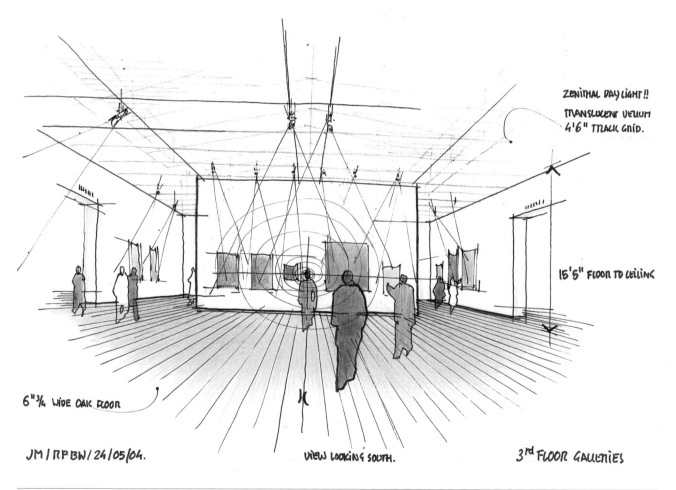

ZENITHAL DAY LIGHT !!
TRANSLUCENT VELLUM
4'6" TRACK GRID.

15'5" FLOOR TO CEILING

6"¾ WIDE OAK FLOOR

JM / RPBW / 24/05/04.   VIEW LOOKING SOUTH.   3rd FLOOR GALLERIES

29

11. Perspective sketch of third-floor galleries

30

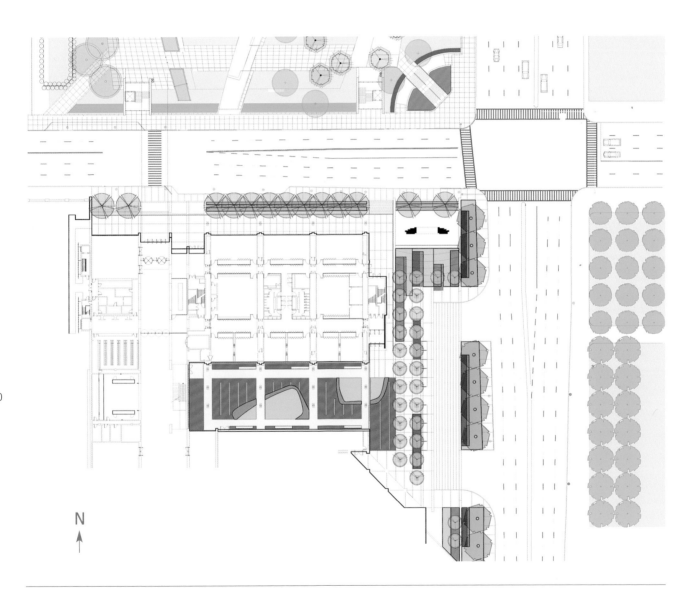

N

12. Site plan showing the proposed landscape design by Gustafson Guthrie Nichol Ltd.

SOUTH GARDEN

12/09/03

13. Perspective view into the garden court between the east pavilion and Rubloff Auditorium

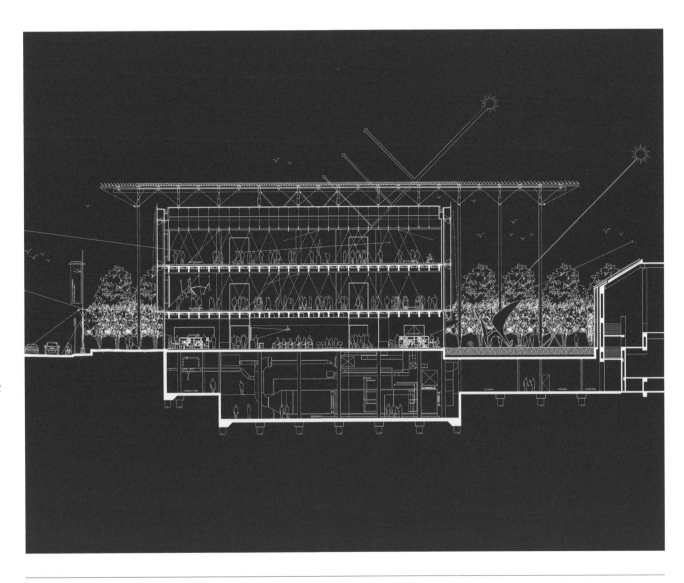

14. North–south section through the east pavilion and garden court, looking east

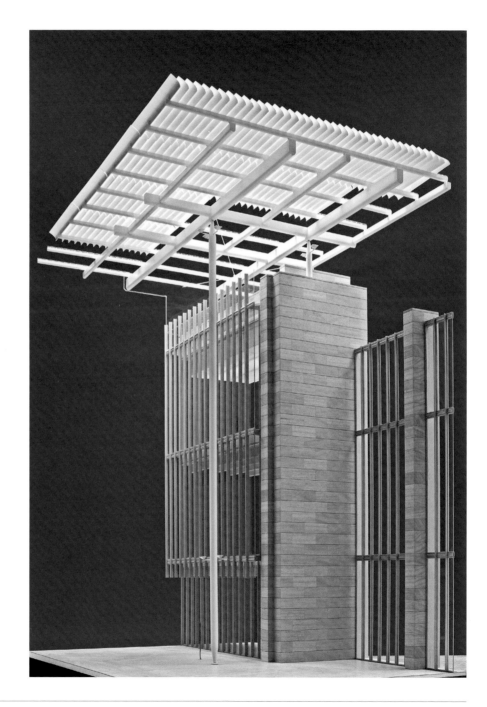

33

34

16. Model of the "flying carpet" roof as seen from below

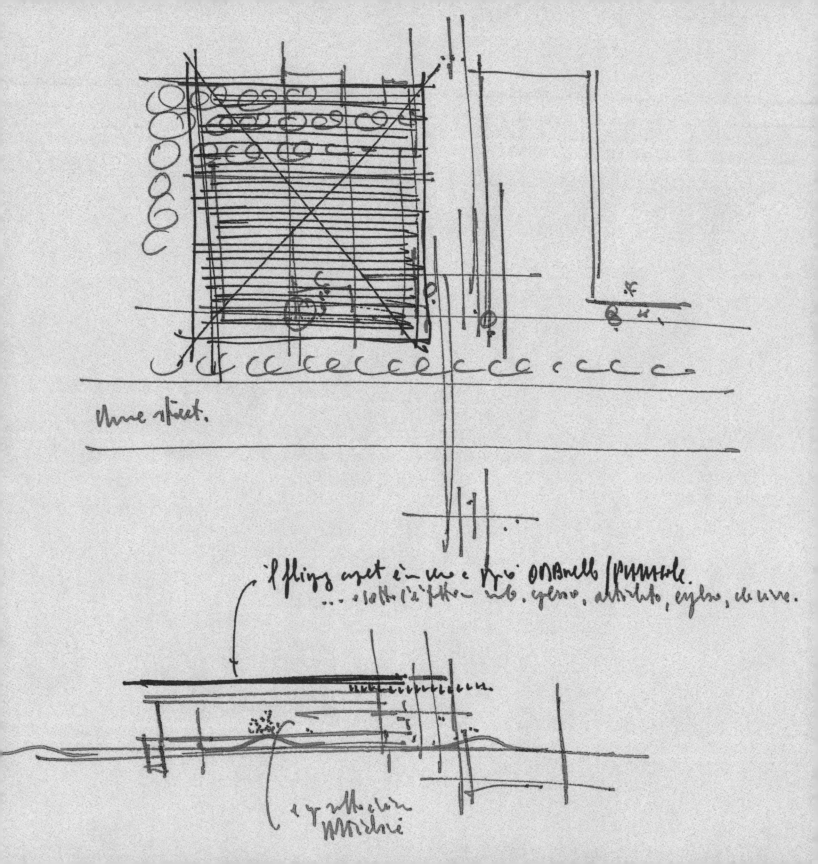

THERE ARE FEW PUBLIC BUILDING commissions of late that have elicited as much attention and debate as those of museums. In the last thirty years, over five hundred new museums of various types have been built in the United States and an even larger number in Europe.[1] Projects to design new museum buildings or additions to existing ones have attracted the foremost architects of our time, perhaps because they offer such unique challenges and rewards. These coveted commissions present the opportunity of creating for enlightened patrons important, highly visible public architecture while at the same time realizing a space to house culturally significant collections of art and other artifacts. Philip Johnson called the museum an architect's dream: "He has—as in a church—to to put [the visitor] in a receptive frame of mind while he is under-going an emotional experience. We architects welcome the challenge."[2] The significance of museums as cultural, civic, and even spiritual institutions has led them to be called cathedrals of the twentieth century.

Museums also represent a building type that has evolved greatly throughout history and is still changing. In addition to their traditional functions of collecting, preserving, studying, and exhibiting works of art, museums must respond to more quotidian needs through cafés, shops, lecture halls, and other services. Institutions face increasing pressure to compete with different types of leisure activities for attracting visitors and they must carefully attend to matters of economic stability if they are to remain viable. The debate around museum architecture and its goals has been especially lively in the recent past.[3] While some architects and critics believe that architecture should position itself at the service of the art to be displayed, others feel that it should engage in a dialogue with art or that the design

BUILDING MUSEUMS FOR THE TWENTY-FIRST CENTURY

Martha Thorne
Associate Curator of Architecture

of the building itself should be viewed as a work of art, on par with the objects displayed inside. There are also larger, civic factors in play. Some new museum buildings are asked to do what even ambitious urban renewal programs could not—generate an urban renaissance in the center of cities. Such was the case with Frank Gehry's highly successful Guggenheim Museum Bilbao, which opened in 1997. The wide-ranging diversity in the discourse about museums and architecture reveals that there is no single ideal. All art institutions celebrate works of art, house them, care for them, and make them available for public appreciation, but beyond this there are a multitude of differences.

Architect Renzo Piano and his firm, Renzo Piano Building Workshop, with offices in Genoa and Paris, can be seen as occupying a pivotal place within the panorama of contemporary museum design in terms of the prominence, quality, and sheer number of their commissions. From his winning competition entry with British architect Richard Rogers for the Centre Georges Pompidou in Paris (1971; completed in 1978) to his current plans for a 260,000-square-foot

FIG. 1 Renzo Piano at the Art Institute of Chicago, showing a model of the roof design for the new north wing

addition to the Art Institute of Chicago, Piano's work reveals a creative and evolving approach to the changing nature of art museums. To date he has designed a long list of museum buildings for over a dozen institutions in eight countries.

The Pompidou Center clearly signaled a break with the past and with the more traditional concept of the museum as simply a building for conserving and displaying great works of art (fig. 2). Piano and Rogers intended this institution, located in the middle of Paris on a cleared former market site, Les Halles, to be a flexible, responsive container for evolving culture. The building was turned inside out, with vibrant color-coded mechanical systems running along the exterior, allowing the interior to be a kind of open "loft." The large floor plates could be divided to create different types of space: galleries for the display of paintings and sculpture, libraries, performance areas, and installations. Perhaps the most important aspect of the Pompidou Center was its mission as a cultural catalyst. Through its bold architecture, it expressed a new idea for a museum that embraced popular culture and

FIG. 2 Centre Georges Pompidou, Paris, 1978, designed by Renzo Piano and Richard Rogers

debunked the concept of art as the purview of the elite. The adjacent piazza—a gathering place, a site of impromptu performances, and an extension of the building itself—also underscored the notion of inclusiveness and accessibility. Finally, the great escalators enclosed in transparent tubes along the facade made the ride up and down an integral part of experiencing the architecture, the building, and the city, thus blurring the line between content, container, and surroundings as never before.

Although the Pompidou Center may have marked Piano's most startling challenge to the traditional past, his other museum buildings have responded to the changing nature of art institutions in equally significant, if subtler, ways. It is interesting to note how Piano's own concerns and ideas about museums recur and evolve from one project to the next. He, of course, works in close concert with the client, seeking to understand and realize the goals set out in the functional program and mission statement of the institution. Using that as one of the cornerstones of his approach, he then calls on his own vocabulary, interests, and repertoire of experiences to create the new design.

FIG. 3 The Menil Collection, Houston, 1987; exterior view showing ferro-cement roof "leaves" and cypress cladding

The site, in the broadest terms, is always a fundamental concern for Piano and a starting point for any proposal. He has demonstrated his sensitivity to setting and his desire to create a dialogue between buildings and their environments in several of his museum commissions, such as the Menil Collection in Houston (1987), the Beyeler Foundation Museum near Basel, Switzerland (1997), and the Nasher Sculpture Center, Dallas (2003). The location of the Menil Collection in a residential neighborhood, with museum functions even occupying some houses in the surrounding area, guided Piano as he designed the building and considered the materials to be used. The resulting two-story structure, clad in cypress siding, fits naturally into its setting; only the distinctive leaf forms of the protruding flat roof signal its unique purpose (see fig. 3). The Beyeler Foundation Museum (fig. 4) at first glance appears to be simply set on an open stretch of land, but it is actually carefully integrated into the location. Inspired by an existing sandstone wall, Piano nestled the building down into the landscape, enclosing its eastern side with a new wall of a similar red color. A winter garden runs along much of the western facade, which

FIG. 4 Beyeler Foundation Museum, Riehen, Switzerland, 1997; exterior view showing the southern porch where a pond extends under the overhanging roof

overlooks a rolling meadow, and allows a meaningful connection to the bucolic backdrop. Piano approached the challenging site of the Nasher Sculpture Center in a different way (see figs. 5–6). The museum is set in the center of the city with a freeway to the north and office towers to the south. Faced with the difficulty of creating a rather small pavilion within a bustling downtown, Piano lined the building up with the street in an urban gesture. While its size and architecture are modest compared to nearby structures, its placement on the site made a direct statement about its role in the city and saved the maximum amount of open land for Peter Walker's sculpture garden.

The new north wing for the Art Institute of Chicago posed several unique challenges: the height limitations imposed on the museum's buildings in accordance with city ordinances for Grant Park; the current complicated floor plan and diverse architectural styles, a result of its incremental growth over more than a hundred years; and the active railroad tracks at the center of the property. Piano drew upon the strengths of the setting: the location selected at the northeast corner of the campus allowed a direct

FIG. 5 Nasher Sculpture Center, Dallas, 2003; aerial view
FIG. 6 View through Giacometti gallery in the Nasher Sculpture Center on to garden

connection with the activities in Millennium Park, which could even be seen as a sort of front yard of the new building. The quality of northern light and the possibility of views toward the park led to the design of a glass facade for the Monroe Street elevation. The airy but rectilinear and fairly stately Art Institute wing will provide a striking contrast to the exuberant, free-form band shell designed by Frank Gehry. Piano's regularly shaped addition accepts the city's rigid street grid, lining up with Monroe Street and Columbus Drive. The clear expression of the structure of the building and the selection of materials (especially the soft-toned Indiana limestone) are in the spirit of Chicago's architectural tradition and in harmony with the existing Art Institute edifices.

While Piano was inspired by specific needs and conditions in his design for the Art Institute building, he also drew upon elements and themes he had developed in previous projects. Fond of using metaphors to describe aspects of his architecture, Piano has likened the organization of space within the north wing to that of a village. As in a village, some activities transpire in the public realm while others remain private. He used a similar analogy in describing the Menil Collection, although the plan there was different in many respects.[4] Piano's concern with finding a delicate balance between the

"sacred" and "profane" missions of the art museum (see essay by James Cuno, p. 12) is also a recurrent theme, aligned with the idea of the "private" and the "public." In the Art Institute plan, the most profane elements (shop, ticket counters, cloakroom) are located near the entrance. As one proceeds along the "main street," the central glass-enclosed concourse, it is possible to branch off on "side streets" and enter galleries, the "sacred" realm of the museum. This idea of movement and the layering of functions has been employed in other Piano buildings. A look at the floor plan for the Menil Collection shows how the galleries are all located off a straight, main axis that extends almost the entire length of the building (see fig. 7). The further one ventures off the promenade, the more tranquil the viewing experience. The glass at either end of the main axis, however, along with the inclusion of courtyards or small garden spaces viewed from the inside (see fig. 8), keeps the visitor in continual contact with the outside and provides an orienting factor.

In his design for the Art Institute, Piano has carefully created connections between interior and exterior that are both poetic and comfortable. The first-floor facade on Monroe Street is transparent, reinforcing the museum's place in the

41

FIG. 7 Interior "promenade" in the Menil Collection
FIG. 8 View from gallery in the Menil Collection into the interior courtyard

heart of the city. The double skin of glass continues on the upper floors, providing views of Millennium Park, the skyline, and the lake, although exhibition panels and translucent screens can be set in front of the windows when gallery spaces need to be enclosed. To the south, between the east pavilion and Rubloff Auditorium, a new garden courtyard designed by landscape architects Gustafson Guthrie Nichol will function almost as an exterior gallery, which visitors can view from the first floor and the stairs leading up to the second floor (see pls. 12–13). By offering glimpses through the galleries to the outside, Piano allows the visitors to orient themselves in time and space, and gives them the opportunity to pause and contemplate the art formed by nature. The garden also provides a connection from the outside in, especially for those pedestrians walking along Columbus Drive or leaving the Lurie Garden of Millennium Park, which was also designed by Gustafson Guthrie Nichol.

Another important component of all of Piano's recent museum designs is light. Buildings that house collections of art are challenged to protect those works from potential light damage, while creating a setting that allows the objects to be viewed in optimal conditions. At times in the development of the modern museum, curators and conservators argued for neutral, enclosed gallery spaces provided with purely artificial lighting that could be minutely controlled and made completely uniform. Today, museum experts rely on a combination of natural and artificial light; the subtle changes in illumination throughout the day and night enrich the viewing experience.

Working with specialized engineers, Piano has developed a number of strategies to perfect the quality of light in his museums. In the Menil Collection building and the nearby Cy Twombly Gallery (completed in 1995), Piano carefully employed light as one of the defining elements of the architecture. The visually dominant roof of the Menil Collection, with its three hundred curved ferro-cement "leaves" that protrude beyond the edge of the building, functions not only as a symbolic "call to attention" but also as a technical invention to filter and direct natural light. Baffles hung below skylights are angled to catch light from the

FIG. 9 Cy Twombly Gallery, Houston, 1995; interior view showing sailcloth layer of lighting system
FIG. 10 Roof of the Cy Twombly Gallery

north and reflect it into the galleries. In the Twombly pavilion, the light from above is filtered through four layers. As it passes through a final layer, that of sail-cloth, and reaches the galleries, it takes on a luminescence that varies ever so subtly depending on outside conditions (see fig. 9). The paintings are viewed in the absence of shadows. From the outside, the roof canopy appears to float above the building (see fig. 10).

In the Beyeler Foundation Museum the architect again highlighted the roof and further developed his floating filter. Composed of angled white glass panels, a layer of flat glass, and computer-controlled motorized louvers that further mediate the incoming light, the floating roof employs sophisticated technology and engineering in the service of art. As a design element, it expresses the importance of sheltering and protecting the works inside the building and creates an interesting dialogue with the rest of the structure. The contrast of the light roof with the heavy and solidly anchored building serves to highlight the specific qualities of each—a technique often used by the architect (see fig. 11).

FIG. 11 Detail of the roof of the Beyeler Foundation Museum

Piano has described the visible roof for the Art Institute that hovers above the building as a "flying carpet." It measures 216 feet square and will extend beyond the perimeter of the building, resting on slender steel columns. The roof is an important symbolic element, granting a more monumental character to the new building and effectively marking the territory of the museum. Its central function, however, is to capture and filter natural light. Rows of beautiful curved "blades" running from east to west along the gridlike structure of the roof shield the galleries, while reflecting natural light through the glass roof over the third floor and into the new courtyard garden. The blades (see figs. 12–13) are made of extruded aluminum and painted a light metallic color, creating a dialogue with the stainless steel Pritzker Pavilion across the street in Millennium Park. Piano has said that while the music pavilion expresses its definition of space through sound, the Art Institute's new building expresses it through light.

The design for the Art Institute of Chicago represents a further refinement of Piano's concern for the integration of building and site, in terms of physical

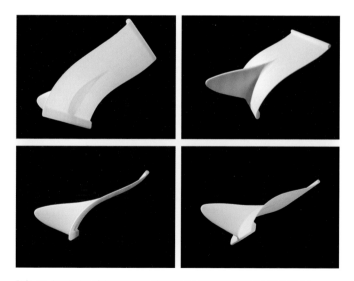

FIG. 12 Installation of the prototype of the "flying carpet" roof for the Art Institute's new north wing in Turin, Italy, January 2002
FIG. 13 Lamella model for the "flying carpet" roof

conditions, local architectural traditions, and institutional identity. While he exercises to the fullest his role as architect, as participant in the making of contemporary culture, he never allows his personal style to overwhelm the unique character and context of the museum. Piano strikes that delicate balance between the sacred, personal nature of art and the need to provide for the more mundane needs of visitors, striving to make his building understandable, enjoyable, and comfortable while keeping art and its contemplation at the forefront. The robust north wing of the Art Institute will express the sturdy nature of the institution and its mission to protect the art inside. But it will also engage with its surroundings, and, if the proposed pedestrian bridge comes to fruition (see Cuno, p. 16), it will symbolically and literally reach out to the city beyond. Piano's design for the Art Institute is thoroughly of its time, employing a modern vocabulary and technologies that position it in the twenty-first century. It is a building that above all expresses balance: between monumentality and human scale, newness and timelessness, function and art, the museum and the city.

NOTES

1. Victoria Newhouse, *Towards a New Museum* (Monacelli Press, 1998), p. 12.

2. Philip Johnson, "Letter to the Museum Director," *Museum News* 38, no. 5 (Jan. 1960), p. 22.

3. See, for example, Newhouse (note 1); Douglas Davis, *The Museum Transformed: Design and Culture in the Post-Pompidou Age* (Abbeville, 1990); Justin Henderson, *Museum Architecture* (Rockport, 1998); John Coolidge, *Patrons and Architects: Designing Art Museums in the Twentieth Century* (Amon Carter Museum, 1989).

4. In the case of the Menil Collection, the architect likened the museum campus, comprising several buildings, to a village. See Renzo Piano, "The De Menil Collection," *Transactions* 5, no. 2 (1987), p. 45.

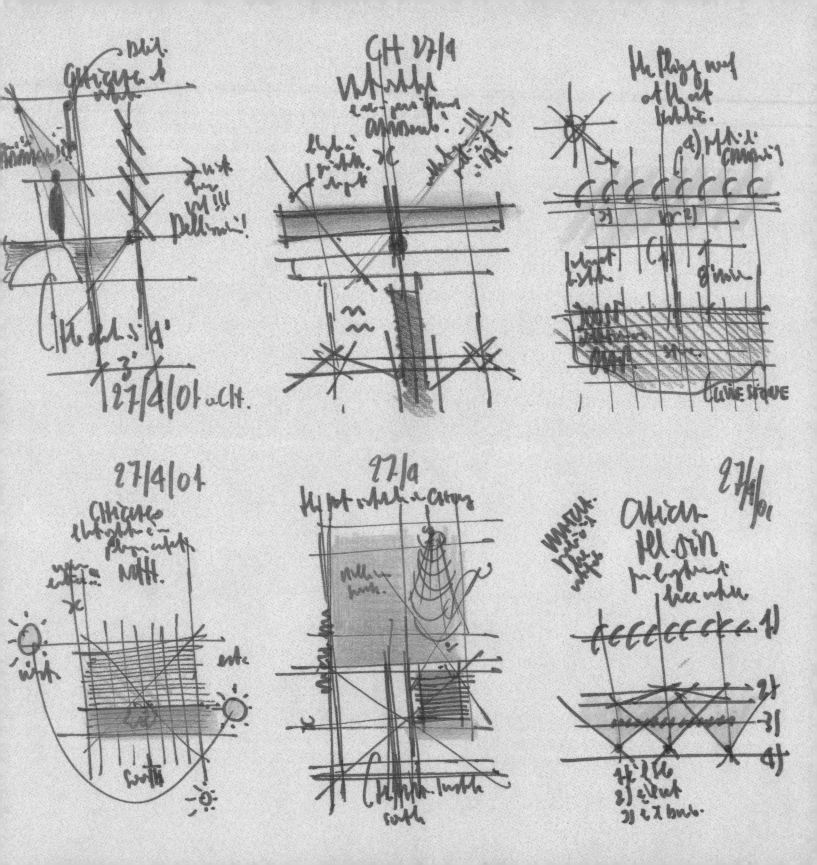

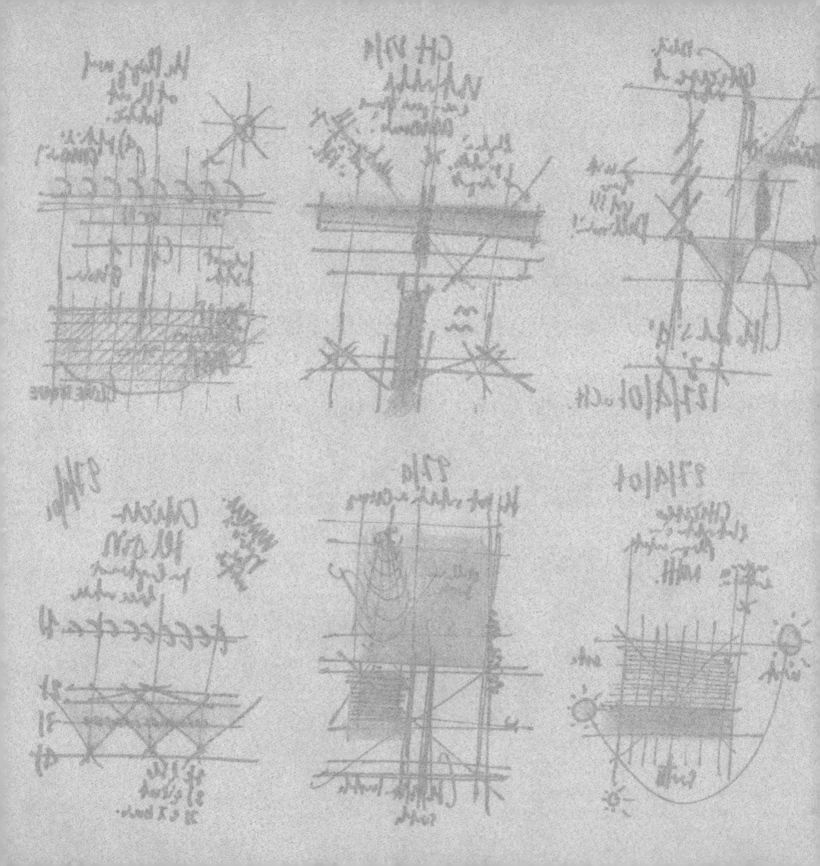

IN MAY 2005 THE ART INSTITUTE OF CHICAGO will break ground on a large addition to open in spring 2009. Designed by Renzo Piano, the north wing will be located on the northeast quadrant of the Art Institute's grounds, with a striking new entrance on Monroe Street. The glass, steel, and limestone structure will add a twenty-first-century architectural identity to a museum best known for its historic Michigan Avenue building. Indiana limestone used for the new wing's west and east elevations will mirror the earlier buildings' materials. The transparency of the north elevation will integrate the interior with the dramatic setting provided by Millennium Park, the city skyline, and Lake Michigan. A luminous sunscreen, described by the architect as a "flying carpet," will "float" above the actual roof and shelter the building and its immediate surroundings, capturing and directing natural light into the third-floor galleries. The "flying carpet," as well as the double curtain wall for the second- and third-story galleries, will reduce the need for artificial lighting and provide a cushion of temperature control; they are among the features that will make the building very energy efficient.

The addition will include approximately 65,000 square feet of gallery space; approximately 20,000 square feet for educational functions; an outdoor sculpture terrace; a glass-enclosed dining facility; and a footbridge to Millennium Park. The street level will be occupied by public functions, including a new shop, a reception area for school groups, and a teacher resource center. A new north–south axis will lead visitors on a "main street" through the building from Monroe Street to the Daniel F. and Ada L. Rice Building. Green space in this area of the campus will be increased by 118 percent, including a new, 11,780-square-foot garden designed by Gustafson Guthrie Nichol of Seattle, Washington. Interactive Design, Chicago, is the associate architect for the building.

PROJECT DESCRIPTION OF THE PROPOSED NEW NORTH WING

Meredith Mack

Vice President for Finance and Operations

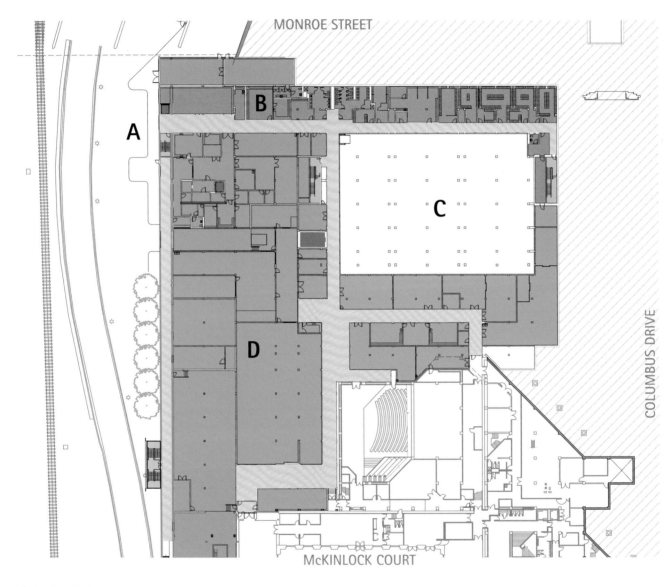

MONROE STREET

A

B

C

D

McKINLOCK COURT

COLUMBUS DRIVE

48

A Loading Dock
B Staff Facilities
C Mechanical Equipment
D Storage

N

GROUND-LEVEL PLAN One floor located below grade will support important museum operations—mechanical functions, storage, and handling. A proposed loading area at the track level will be accessed from Randolph Street to the north, allowing the museum to remove one of its existing service entrances along Monroe Street.

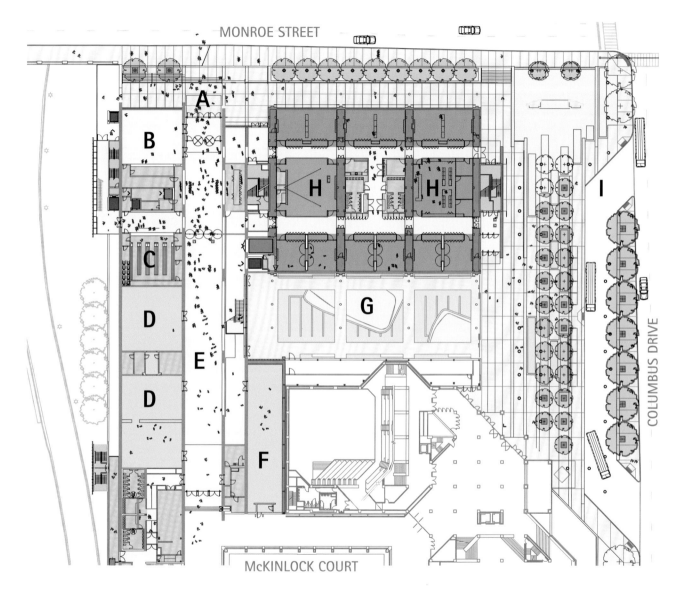

MONROE STREET

A

B

C

D

E

D

F

G

H   H

I

McKINLOCK COURT

COLUMBUS DRIVE

49

A Monroe Street Entrance

B Museum Shop

C Cloakroom

D Temporary Exhibition Galleries

E Main Concourse

F Photography Galleries

G Garden Court

H Museum Education Facilities

I School Bus Drop-off

N

FIRST-FLOOR PLAN Educational functions will receive approximately 20,000 square feet of space on the first floor. School children drop-off will continue to be along Columbus Drive with changes that will enhance landscaping and improve the existing driveway/drop-off area.

MONROE STREET

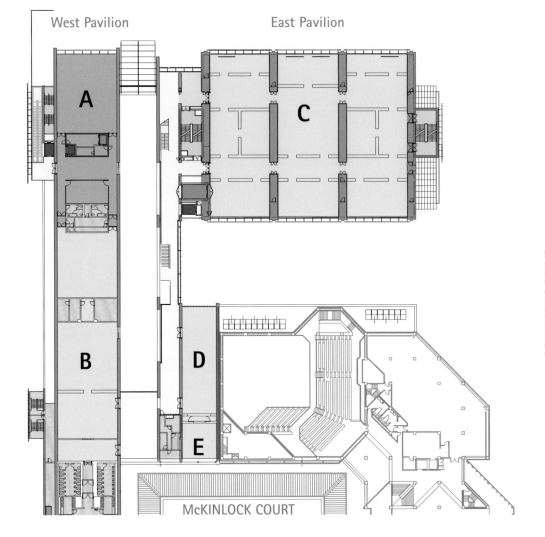

West Pavilion   East Pavilion

A

C

B

D

E

COLUMBUS DRIVE

McKINLOCK COURT

50

A Boardrooms

B Architecture Galleries

C Contemporary Art Galleries

D Contemporary Installation Galleries

E Contemporary Film and Video Space

N

SECOND-FLOOR PLAN The three-story addition will include approximately 65,000 square feet of gallery space for modern and contemporary art: painting, sculpture, photography, film and video, and architecture. Ceiling heights of over 18 feet will accommodate large-scale works of contemporary art.

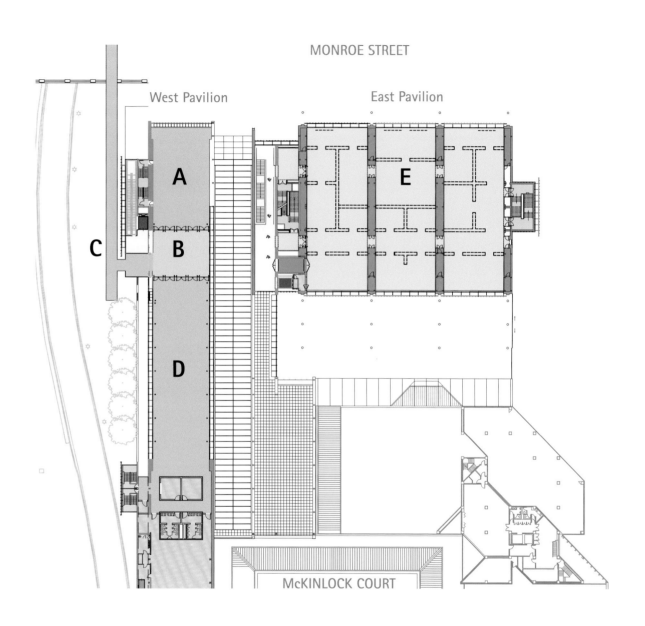

MONROE STREET

West Pavilion

East Pavilion

A

B

C

D

E

McKINLOCK COURT

COLUMBUS DRIVE

A Sculpture Terrace
B Winter Garden
C Pedestrian Bridge
D Dining Facility
E Modern Art Galleries

N

THIRD-FLOOR PLAN The second and third floors of the east pavilion will be devoted exclusively to galleries of art. The most unusual feature of the third floor with be the presence of daylight reflected through the "flying carpet" and illuminating the galleries through the glass roof. A glass-enclosed dining facility and rooftop sculpture terrace are the main features of the west pavilion, with access to Millennium Park via a pedestrian bridge.

NEW NORTH WING
PROJECT TEAM

Design Architect:
Renzo Piano Building Workshop, Paris

Associate Architect:
Interactive Design, Chicago

Engineer:
Ove Arup, London

Landscape Architect:
Gustafson Guthrie Nichol Ltd., Seattle

Program Manager:
The Rise Group, Chicago

Site Utilities Engineer:
Patrick Engineering Inc., Chicago

Electrical Engineer:
Jose de Avila and Associates, Oak Park

Construction Management:
Turner, Chicago

Mechanical Systems Engineer:
Sebesta Blomberg and Associates, Chicago

Commissioning and LEED Consultant:
Carter Burgess, Chicago

Zero Gravity: The Art Institute, Renzo Piano, and Building for a New Century has been published in conjunction with an exhibition organized by the Renzo Piano Building Workshop and the Art Institute of Chicago and presented from May 31 to October 2, 2005.

First edition
Printed in the United States of America

Published by
The Art Institute of Chicago
111 South Michigan Avenue
Chicago, Illinois 60603-6110
www.artic.edu

Library of Congress Control Number:
2005923394
ISBN 0-86559-219-5

Produced by the Publications Department of the Art Institute of Chicago, Susan F. Rossen, Executive Director
Edited by Robert V. Sharp and Katherine E. Reilly
Production by Amanda W. Freymann
Designed and typeset by Karin Kuzniar, Department of Graphic Design, and Photographic and Communications Services
Separations by Professional Graphics, Rockford, Illinois; printing and binding by Original Smith Printing, Bloomington, Illinois

Photography Credits

opp. pp. 6, 9, 13 (bottom), 16, 24-25: The Art Institute of Chicago, Department of Graphic Design, and Photographic and Communications Services, photography by Robert Lifson and Bob Hashimoto; pp. 5, 36, 45 (top): The Art Institute of Chicago

p. 40: Courtesy of the Nasher Sculpture Center, photography by Tim Hursley

All other photographs © Renzo Piano Building Workshop, including pp. 19 (top), 22, 37, 39, 42 (top), 44: photography by Michel Denoncé; p. 34: photography by Francesca Avanzinelli; pp. 38, 42 (bottom), 43: photography by Hickey & Robertson

Front cover: sketch by Renzo Piano of Monroe Street elevation of the north wing; back cover: pl. 15; p. 2: partial section of the east pavilion; vellum inserts: concept sketches for the new north wing by Renzo Piano, 2000–01: insert opp. p. 6: The Art Institute of Chicago, gift of Renzo Piano, 2001.571.